FAMILY TIES

FAMILY TIES

A Message for Fathers

L. TOM PERRY

DESERET
BOOK

Salt Lake City, Utah

© 2011 L. Tom Perry

DESERET BOOK is a registered trademark of Deseret Book Company.

Visit us at DeseretBook.com

Library of Congress Cataloging-in-Publication Data
(CIP on file)
ISBN 978-1-60908-768-5

Printed in the United States of America
Publishers Printing, Salt Lake City, UT

10   9   8   7   6   5   4   3   2   1

CONTENTS

❖

Parents have a sacred duty to rear their children
in love and righteousness, to provide for their physical
and spiritual needs, to teach them to love and serve one
another, to observe the commandments of God and
to be law-abiding citizens wherever they live.

The Family: A Proclamation to the World

Chapter One

Husbands and Fathers— Your Roles and Responsibilities

❖

The Book of Mormon tells a remarkable story about a father who loved his son so much he gave him his own name. The father was chief high priest in the land and spent much of his days administering to the spiritual needs of the people. How disappointed he must have been when his son chose to turn from his teachings.

As any righteous father would, he pleaded with the Lord for a change to occur in the life of his son. In answer to his prayers, an angel stood before this young man and said, "Behold, the Lord hath heard the prayers of his people, and also the prayers of his servant, Alma, who is thy father; for he has prayed with much faith concerning thee that thou mightest be brought to a knowledge of the truth" (Mosiah 27:14).

The scriptures record how the prayers of a righteous father were answered. History attests to the power of righteous leadership in the home.

I want to focus on those who bear the great and noble titles of husband and father. I find myself greatly concerned with what I see around me. Man, woman, young adult, youth, and child—all groping to find their identity in a troubled world. Husbands and fathers, may I again remind you of your roles and your responsibilities?

First, as a husband: The first instruction given to man and woman immediately following the Creation was, "Therefore shall a man leave his father and his mother, and shall cleave unto his wife: and they shall be one flesh" (Genesis 2:24).

So God in His divine plan ordained that marriage was to bring about His basic organizational unit—the family. The roles of husband and wife were clearly defined from the very beginning. In the Lord's plan, these roles are unchanged and eternal.

A prophet has said of womanhood, "A beautiful, modest, gracious woman is creation's masterpiece."[1]

To safeguard this masterpiece, the Lord gave to man the duty and responsibility to be the provider and protector. Husbands, if the Lord's plan is to be accomplished, you must learn how to perform in the leadership role He has designed for you. May I remind you of some of these requirements?

First, let me share an experience related by Sister Emma Rae McKay, wife of President David O. McKay. She shared it many years ago, but it is even more relevant today:

"Last summer on reaching Los Angeles, we decided to have our car washed by one of those 'Quickies' on Wilshire Boulevard.

"As I was watching the last part of the operation from a bench, to my surprise a tiny voice at my elbow said, 'I guess that man over there loves you.'

"I turned and saw a beautiful little curly-haired child with great brown eyes who looked to be about seven years of age.

"'What did you say?' I asked.

"'I said, I guess that man over there loves you.'

"'Oh, yes, he loves me; he is my husband. But why do you ask?'

"A tender smile lighted up his face and his voice softened as he said, 'Cuz, the way he smiled at you. Do you know I'd give anything in this world if my pop would smile at my mom that way.'

"'Oh, I'm sorry if he doesn't.'

"'I guess you're not going to get a divorce,' he [questioned me].

"'No, of course not; we've been married over fifty years. Why do you ask that?'

"'Cuz everybody gets a divorce around here. My pop is getting a divorce from my mom, and I love my pop and I love my mom. . . .'

"His voice broke, and tears welled up in his eyes, but he was too much of a little man to let them fall.

"'Oh, I'm sorry to hear that!'

"And then he came very close and whispered confidentially into my ear, 'You'd better hurry out of this place or you'll get a divorce, too!'"[2]

Husbands, are your actions at all times a reflection of

your love for your wife? If that had been you at the carwash, would that little boy have noticed the same tender love in so much abundance?

Second, it is your responsibility to provide peace and security in your home. It is your duty to provide adequately for your family. You must prepare yourself for this responsibility and have the ambition to see that it is accomplished. Your wife should live her life with the comforting assurance that so long as you are healthy and well, you will take care of her first above all others.

Third, it is a 24/7 job to respect your eternal companion. There is too much unrighteous leadership being exercised in too many marriages. The Lord has warned us in the scriptures by saying:

"We have learned by sad experience that it is the nature and disposition of almost all men, as soon as they get a little authority, as they suppose, they will immediately begin to exercise unrighteous dominion. . . .

"No power or influence can or ought to be maintained by virtue of the priesthood, only by persuasion, by long-suffering, by gentleness and meekness, and by love unfeigned" (D&C 121:39, 41).

Your wife is your companion, your best friend, your full partner. The Lord has blessed her with great potential, talent, and ability. She, too, must be given the opportunity for self-expression and development. Her happiness should be your greatest concern. Learn how to magnify both your roles in order that both husband and wife can be found having fulfilling and happy lives together.

Brethren, your first and most responsible role in life and in the eternities is to be a righteous husband.

Second only to the title of husband is that of father. Next to eternal life, the greatest of all gifts that our Father in Heaven can bestow on a man is the opportunity of being blessed with sons and daughters. Every healthy and normal son of God should have the joy of bestowing the following gifts on his children:

First, an honored and respected name. I will be eternally grateful to a father who thought enough of me to give me his name. It was a name of honor and respect in the community in which I grew up. It carried before it the title of bishop from the time I was six months old until just a few months before I left to go on my mission.

How proud I was of his service. I was pleased that he had the patience to involve me in his responsibilities. Working on a welfare farm, cleaning the chapel, balancing ward financial records, carrying a sack of flour to a widow, and other opportunities for service, were a part of my early life. I was with him so much I received the nickname of "Bishop." I attempted to wear it with pride and honor. It had the effect of making me reach a little higher. I wanted to try to be on the same plane as my father. Should not every child have the same opportunity?

Fathers, it is your obligation to give your children an honored and respected name.

Second, every child needs a sense of security. I often think of the security of our old family home. It was a fortress against the adversary. Each morning and evening it was blessed by the priesthood as we would kneel in family prayer. That power was also manifest as my father blessed his family in time of need.

Fathers, is it not your obligation to give your children a home blessed with the power of the priesthood?

Third, children need their father's time and attention. My children taught me a great lesson many years ago. Our family had moved from California to New York, where I had accepted a position with a new company. We began the process of finding a new home by looking in communities closest to the city. Gradually, however, we moved farther away from the city to find a home in a neighborhood that suited our needs. We found a beautiful home some distance from New York City. It was a one-story house nestled in the lovely deep woods of Connecticut. The final test before purchasing the home was for me to ride the commuter train into New York and check the time and see how long the commute would take. I made the trip and returned quite discouraged. The trip was one and one-half hours each way. I walked into our motel room where our family was waiting for me and presented a choice to my children.

"You can have either this house or a father," I said. Much to my surprise they responded, "We'll take the house. You're never around much anyway." I was devastated. What my children were telling me was true. I needed to repent fast. My children needed a father who was home more. Eventually we reached a compromise and bought a home closer to the city, with a much shorter commute. I changed my work habits to allow me to have more time with my family.

Fourth, give your children the opportunity of having a joyful, happy childhood. I'm reminded of a story written many years ago by Bryant S. Hinckley. It is as follows:

"Three hundred twenty-six school children of a district near Indianapolis were asked to write anonymously just what each thought of his father.

"The teacher hoped that the reading of the essays might attract the fathers to attend at least one meeting of the Parent-Teachers Association.

"It did.

"They came in $400 cars and $4,000 cars. Bank president, laborer, professional man, clerk, salesman, meter reader, farmer, utility magnate, merchant, baker, tailor, manufacturer, and contractor, every man with a definite estimate of himself in terms of money, skill, and righteousness. . . .

"The president picked at random from another stack of papers. 'I like my daddy,' she read from each. The reasons were many: he built my doll house, took me coasting, taught me to shoot, helps with my schoolwork, takes me to the park, gave me a pig to fatten and sell. Scores of essays could be reduced to 'I like my daddy. He plays with me.'

"Not one child mentioned his family house, car, neighborhood, food, or clothing.

"The fathers went into the meeting from many walks of life; they came out in two classes: companions to their children or strangers to their children.

"No man is too rich or too poor to play with his children."[3]

I am aware how concerned we each are with the leadership we find in the world today. To change the head of a nation, state, or community toward righteous leadership may require our earnest efforts for years. But there is something we can change today to make the world a better place in which to live. Husbands and fathers, the power is within you as bearers of the priesthood. Enjoy the inspiration of God, our Eternal Father, to lead, guide, and direct your families in righteousness. You stand at the head of the only organization I know of that can be eternal. Should not that charge and responsibility receive top priority in your life?

God bless you to understand your roles and responsibilities to be righteous husbands and fathers.

Chapter Two

CALLED OF GOD

The fifth article of faith states, "We believe that a man must be called of God, by prophecy, and by the laying on of hands by those who are in authority, to preach the Gospel and administer in the ordinances thereof" (Articles of Faith 1:5).

One of our most important priesthood callings, one that requires our constant attention, is in our families and our homes. Brethren, as fathers and patriarchs in our families, we are "by divine design . . . to preside over [our] families in love and righteousness and are . . . to provide the necessities of life and protection for [our] families." Moreover, "husband and wife have a solemn responsibility to love and care for each other and for their children. . . . Parents have a sacred duty to rear their children in love and righteousness, to provide for their physical and spiritual needs, to teach them to love and serve one another, to observe the commandments of God and to be law-abiding citizens wherever they live. Husbands and wives—mothers and fathers—will be held accountable before God for the discharge of these obligations."[1]

We live in a world that is crying for righteous leadership based on trustworthy principles.

In our Church we have been taught, in our own unique way, correct principles of leadership, directed by priesthood authority. I believe few of us realize the potential of the priesthood and the blessing it is. The more we learn about holding the priesthood and understand its operation, the more we appreciate the blessings the Lord has given to us.

President John Taylor once declared:

"I shall . . . briefly answer that [the priesthood] is the government of God, whether on the earth or in the heavens, for it is by that power, agency, or principle that all things are [upheld and] governed on the earth and in the heavens, and [it is] by that power that all things are upheld and sustained. It governs all things—it directs all things—it sustains all things—and has to do with all things that God and truth are associated with.

"It is the power of God delegated to intelligences in the heavens and to men on the earth . . . ; and when we arrive in the celestial kingdom of God, we shall find the most perfect order and harmony existing, because there is the perfect pattern, the most perfect order of government carried out, and when or wherever those principles have been developed in the earth, in proportion as they have spread and been acted upon, just in that proportion have they produced blessings and salvation to the human family; and when the government of God shall be more extensively adopted, and when Jesus' prayer, that He taught His disciples is answered, and God's kingdom comes on the earth, and His will is done here as in heaven, then, and not till then, will universal love, peace, harmony, and union prevail."[2]

The Lord gave us a vision of what the priesthood can be as He directed His Apostles, who were to carry on the work following His death. He declared to them, "Ye have not chosen me, but I have chosen you, and ordained you, that ye should go and bring forth fruit, and that your fruit should remain: that whatsoever ye shall ask of the Father in my name, he may give it you" (John 15:16).

One of the blessings received from the priesthood is having the opportunity of belonging to a quorum. A quorum of the priesthood consists of a specific group of men holding the same priesthood office, organized for the more effective advancement of the kingdom of God.

President Stephen L Richards at one time gave us a threefold definition of a priesthood quorum. He said a priesthood quorum is three things: "first, a class; second, a fraternity; and third, a service unit."[3]

I was taught how a quorum works in these three aspects many years ago when I attended a high priests group meeting in a small community in southern Wyoming. The lesson that week was on justification and sanctification. It was evident, as the lesson began, that the teacher was well prepared to instruct his brethren. Then a question prompted a response that changed the whole course of the lesson. In response to the question, one brother commented: "I have listened with great interest to the lesson material. The thought has crossed my mind that the information presented will soon be lost if we do not find application to put the material presented into practice in our daily lives." Then he went on to propose a course of action.

The night before, a citizen of the community had passed away. His wife was a member of the Church, but he had not been. This high priest had visited the widow and offered his sympathy. Leaving the home after the visit, his eyes wandered over the beautiful farm of the deceased brother. He had put so much of his life and labor into building it up. The alfalfa was ready to cut; the grain would soon be ready to harvest. How would this poor sister cope with the sudden problems now falling on her? She would need time to get herself organized for her new responsibilities.

Then he proposed to the group that they apply the principles they had just been taught—by working with the widow to keep her farm operating until the widow and her family could find a more permanent solution. The balance of the meeting was spent in organizing the project to assist her.

As we left the classroom, there was a good feeling among the brethren. I heard one of them remark as he passed through the doorway, "This project is just what we needed as a group to work together again." A lesson had been taught; a brotherhood had been strengthened; a service project had been organized to assist someone in need.

Now, these principles taught to us in the organization of a quorum apply not only to a quorum but also to the priesthood leadership in the home. We are under divine command to "bring up [our] children in light and truth" (D&C 93:40). If fathers do not raise their children in light and truth, then the Lord is displeased with them. This is the message:

"But verily I say unto you, my servant . . . , you have continued under . . . condemnation;

"You have not taught your children light and truth, according to the commandments; and that wicked one hath power, as yet, over you, and this is the cause of your affliction.

"And now a commandment I give unto you—if you will be delivered you shall set in order your own house, for there are many things that are not right in your house" (D&C 93:41–43).

The Church must retain its family-based orientation. We need to teach the concept of building successive generations of members who are married in the temple and stay faithful. We need to teach basic doctrines and understand the relationship between personal spiritual growth and that of the family. We need to make the outcome clear: inviting members to come unto Christ and endure to the end.

Among the first instructions given to man and woman was, "Therefore shall a man leave his father and his mother, and shall cleave unto his wife; and they shall be one flesh" (Moses 3:24).

God, in His divine plan, ordained marriage to bring about His basic organizational unit—the family. One of the first principles He taught Adam and Eve was to develop a working relationship. The scripture states:

"And Adam and Eve, his wife, called upon the name of the Lord, and they heard the voice of the Lord from the way toward the Garden of Eden, speaking unto them, and they saw him not; for they were shut out from his presence.

"And he gave unto them commandments, that they should worship the Lord their God, and should offer the firstlings of their flocks, for an offering unto the Lord. And Adam was obedient unto the commandments of the Lord" (Moses 5:4–5).

Then the Lord instructed our first earthly parents to teach their children about obedience to His laws, "and Adam and Eve blessed the name of God, and they made all things known unto their sons and their daughters" (Moses 5:12).

President Spencer W. Kimball taught us about the eternal nature of the family:

"The formula is simple; the ingredients are few, though there are many amplifications of each.

"First, there must be the proper approach toward marriage, which contemplates the selection of a spouse who reaches as nearly as possible the pinnacle of perfection in all the matters that are of importance to the individuals. Then those two parties must come to the altar in the temple realizing that they must work hard toward this successful joint living.

"Second, there must be great unselfishness, forgetting self and directing all of the family life and all pertaining thereunto to the good of the family, and subjugating self.

"Third, there must be continued courting and expressions of affection, kindness, and consideration to keep love alive and growing.

"Fourth, there must be complete living of the commandments of the Lord as defined in the gospel of Jesus Christ."[4]

Homes should be an anchor, a safe harbor, a place of refuge, a happy place where families dwell together, a place where children are loved. In the home, parents should teach their children the great lessons of life. Home should be the center of one's earthly experience, where love and mutual respect are appropriately blended.

Throughout the ages, the Lord has commanded His people to teach their children truth and righteousness. We encourage you to gather your families around you for family prayer, gospel study, family work, and family activities. We urge you to counsel with your family members and encourage them to participate in the important decisions.

President Brigham Young taught, "The Priesthood . . . is [the] perfect order and system of government, and this alone can deliver the human family from all the evils which now afflict its members, and insure them happiness and felicity hereafter."[5]

We have been given the great power of the priesthood. It blesses us individually and provides blessings for our family; it blesses the quorums to which we belong; it blesses the congregations in which we are called to serve; and it even blesses the world in which we live. We need to learn how to righteously follow the doctrines and teachings the Lord has given to us as bearers of His holy priesthood. We are counseled:

"Wherefore, now let every man learn his duty, and to act in the office in which he is appointed, in all diligence.

"He that is slothful shall not be counted worthy to stand, and he that learns not his duty and shows himself not approved shall not be counted worthy to stand" (D&C 107:99–100).

May the Lord bless us, as members of His Church,

that we may realize what a blessing it is to have the priesthood on earth and to be able to use it for the benefit of our families and of all mankind. May we grow to understand our relationship to God our Eternal Father and the priesthood He has given to us.

Chapter Three

THE IMPORTANCE
OF THE FAMILY

W e need to make our homes places of refuge from the storm, which is increasing in intensity all about us. Even if the smallest openings are left unattended, negative influences can penetrate the very walls of our homes. Let me cite an example.

Several years ago, I was having dinner with my daughter and her family. The scene is all too common in most homes with small children. My daughter was trying to encourage her three-year-old son to eat a balanced meal. He had eaten all the food on his plate that he liked. A small serving of green beans remained, which he was not fond of. In desperation, his mother picked up a fork and tried to encourage him to eat his beans. He tolerated it just about as long as he could. Then he exclaimed, "Look, Mom, don't foul up a good friendship!"

Those were the exact words he had heard on a television commercial a few days earlier. Oh, what impact advertising, television programs, the Internet, and the other media are having on our family units!

We remind you that parents are to preside over their own families.[1]

Helps and reminders come from the Church Internet site and television channels, as well as through priesthood and auxiliary leadership, to assist us as we strive to fulfill our family responsibilities.

In some of the areas of the world, we have an alternative to commercial television networks and their anti-family programming. We have BYU Television, which presents family-oriented programs. In addition to programs that bring gospel teaching, there are programs directed to parent instruction and family entertainment.

There are other helps that cover a wider area than the television network: we have the Church website, www.lds.org, which includes a home and family page. The page includes thoughts from the scriptures and Church leaders to strengthen the family. It also includes ideas for family activities. A home and family section provides the following:

- Teachings from Church leaders specifically for the family
- Ideas for family activities
- Family home evening quick tips to help you have meaningful and enjoyable family home evenings
- Featured articles on such topics as making family home evenings more successful, strengthening the relationship between husband and wife, and growing closer as family members

We do have one media source, however, that reaches the entire Church—our wonderful Church magazines. These magazines come into our homes regularly and are another way of delivering information to help strengthen the family. Throughout the year, issues of the *Liahona, Ensign, New Era,* and *Friend* contain materials for teaching in the home. There are wonderful suggestions for family home evenings and ideas for everyday teaching moments. The articles are written so they can easily be adapted as lessons for your family.

Children and youth are shown, through prophetic words and through living examples, the importance of loving and honoring their parents. Parents are taught ways of building and maintaining close family ties, both in good times and in difficult times. The good spirit in these magazines will help fill your homes with warmth, love, and the strength of the gospel.

The *Church News* is also helping to spread the message of the family. It has articles on strengthening love and respect in the home, putting the gospel in action, and planning wholesome recreation.

We hope that by flooding the Church with family-oriented media, members of the Church will be assisted and encouraged to build stronger and better families. We hope it will cause a conscious and sustained effort in building an eternal family unit. An abundance of Church materials will be available for you from which to pick and choose useful ideas. At least by seeing family issues mentioned so often, we all will be reminded to focus our attention on the most important organization the Lord has established here on earth.

From the very beginning the Lord has established the importance of the family organization for us. Soon after Adam and Eve left the Garden of Eden, the Lord spoke to them.

"The Holy Ghost fell upon Adam, [and] beareth record of the Father and the Son. . . .

"[Then] in that day Adam blessed God and was filled, and began to prophesy concerning all the families of the earth, saying: Blessed be the name of God, for because of my transgression my eyes are opened, and in this life I shall have joy, and again in the flesh I shall see God.

"And Eve, his wife, heard all these things and was glad, saying: [If it were] not for our transgression we never should have had seed, and never should have known good and evil, and the joy of our redemption, and the eternal life which God giveth unto all the obedient.

"And Adam and Eve blessed the name of God, and they made all things known unto their sons and their daughters" (Moses 5:9–12).

In an earlier edition of the *Gospel Principles* manual

we read the following: "President Brigham Young explained that our families are not yet ours. The Lord has committed them to us to see how we will treat them. Only if we are faithful will they be given to us forever. What we do on earth determines whether or not we will be worthy to become heavenly parents."[2]

The Church has established two special times for families to be together. The first is centered on the proper observance of the Sabbath day. This is the time we are to attend our regular meetings together and study the life and teachings of the Savior and of the prophets. "Other appropriate Sunday activities include (1) writing personal and family journals, (2) holding family councils, (3) establishing and maintaining family organizations for the immediate and extended family, (4) personal interviews between parents and children, (5) writing to relatives and missionaries, (6) genealogy, (7) visiting relatives and those who are ill or lonely, (8) missionary work, (9) reading stories to children, and (10) singing Church hymns."[3]

The second time is Monday night. We are to teach our children in a well-organized, regular family home evening. No other activities should involve our family members on Monday night. This *designated* time is to be with our families.

In an interview with the *Boston Globe,* President Gordon B. Hinckley made the following statement regarding family home evening: "'We have a family home evening program once a week [Monday night] across the Church in which parents sit down with their children. They study the scriptures. They talk about family problems. They plan family activities and things of that kind. I don't hesitate to say if every family in the world practiced that one thing, you'd see a very great difference in the solidarity of the families of the world.'"[4]

A First Presidency letter dated October 4, 1999, bears repeating:

> To: Members of the Church throughout
>   the World
>
> Dear Brothers and Sisters:
>
> Monday nights are reserved throughout the Church for family home evenings. We encourage members to set aside this time to strengthen family ties and teach the gospel in their homes.

Earlier this year we called on parents to devote their best efforts to the teaching and rearing of their children in gospel principles which will keep them close to the Church. We also counseled parents and children to give highest priority to family prayer, family home evening, gospel study and instruction, and wholesome family activities.

We urge members, where possible, to avoid holding receptions or other similar activities on Monday evenings. Where practical, members may also want to encourage community and school leaders to avoid scheduling activities on Monday evenings that require children or parents to be away from their homes.

Church buildings and facilities should be closed on Monday evenings. No ward or stake activities should be planned, and other interruptions to family home evenings should be avoided.[5]

May it be our resolve to build a gospel-centered home, a safe harbor from the storms of the adversary. Let us again remember the promises and instructions from the Lord to His children:

"The glory of God is intelligence, or, in other words, light and truth.

"Light and truth forsake that evil one. . . .

"And that wicked one cometh and taketh away light and truth, through disobedience, from the children of men, and because of the tradition of their fathers.

"But I have commanded you to bring up your children in light and truth" (D&C 93:36–37, 39–40).

My humble prayer is that we may enjoy the light and truth of the gospel in our homes, that our homes may truly become places of refuge from the world.

Chapter Four

Let Him Do It with Simplicity

❖

Those of us who have been around a while have recognized certain patterns in life's test. There are cycles of good and bad times, ups and downs, periods of joy and sadness, and times of plenty as well as scarcity. When our lives turn in an unanticipated and undesirable direction, sometimes we experience stress and anxiety. One of the challenges of this mortal experience is to not allow the stresses and strains of life to get the better of us—to endure the varied seasons of life while remaining positive, even optimistic.

Perhaps when difficulties and challenges strike, we should have these hopeful words of Robert Browning etched in our minds: "The best is yet to be."[1] We can't predict all the struggles and storms in life, not even the ones just around the next corner, but as persons of faith and hope, we know beyond the shadow of any doubt that the gospel of Jesus Christ is true and the best is yet to come.

I remember a particular period of my life when I was under unusual stress. There were troubles with my employment, and at the same time, my wife was diagnosed with a life-threatening illness. This was one of those times when it felt like the adversary had mounted a frontal assault against me and my family. On days when the stresses and anxieties of our tumultuous life were about to get the best of us, my wife and I found a way to relieve them.

We drove to a place a few miles from our home to get away for a few moments of relief from our troubles, to talk and give emotional comfort to each other. Our place was Walden Pond. It was a beautiful little pond surrounded by forests of trees. When my wife was feeling strong enough, we'd go for a walk around the pond. Other days, when she did not feel up to the exertion of walking, we'd just sit in the car and talk. Walden Pond was our special place to pause, reflect, and heal. Perhaps it was partly due to its history—its connection to the efforts of Henry David Thoreau to separate himself from worldliness for a period of years—that Walden Pond offered us so much hope for simplicity and provided such a renewing escape from our overly complex lives.

It was in March of 1845 that Thoreau decided to move out on the banks of Walden Pond and spend two years trying to figure out what life was all about. He settled on a piece of property owned by his good friend Ralph Waldo Emerson. He purchased an old shanty from a railroad worker and tore it down. From the lumber from the shanty and the lumber from the woods, he constructed his own cabin. He kept meticulous financial records, and he concluded that for a home and freedom he spent a mere $28.12. He planted a garden, where he sowed peas, potatoes, corn, beans, and turnips to help sustain his simple life. He planted two and a half acres of beans with the intent of using the small profit to cover his needs. Small profit indeed: $8.71.

Thoreau lived quite independent of time. He had

neither a clock nor a calendar in his little cabin. He spent his time writing and studying the beauties and wonder of nature that surrounded him, including local plants, birds, and animals. He did not live the life of a hermit—he visited the town of Concord most days, and he invited others to come into his cabin for enlightening conversations. When the two years ended, he left his cabin behind without regret. He considered the time he had spent there a proper amount of time to accomplish his purpose—to experience the spiritual benefits of a simplified lifestyle. He also felt he had other life experiences ahead of him. It was time to move on and explore other opportunities.

From his experiences at Walden Pond, Thoreau determined that there were only four things that a man really needed: food, clothing, shelter, and fuel. I would like to expand on each of these four basic needs of life, as well as the spiritual benefits of a simplified lifestyle.

The first requirement is food. As members of The Church of Jesus Christ of Latter-day Saints, we possess sacred knowledge from revealed truth about the relationship between the body and the spirit. Doctrine and Covenants 88:15 states, "The spirit and the body are the soul of man." To bless us both physically and spiritually, the Lord also revealed to us a law of health, telling us which foods and substances are good for the body and which are not. With these instructions comes the promise found in section 89 of the Doctrine and Covenants:

"And all saints who remember to keep and do these sayings, walking in obedience to the commandments, shall receive health in their navel and marrow to their bones;

"And shall find wisdom and great treasures of knowledge, even hidden treasures;

"And shall run and not be weary, and shall walk and not faint.

"And I, the Lord, give unto them a promise, that the destroying angel shall pass by them, as the children of Israel, and not slay them" (verses 18–21).

There is no better counsel concerning the Word of Wisdom than that found in the booklet *For the Strength of Youth.* It states:

"The Lord has commanded you to take good care of your body. To do this, observe the Word of Wisdom, found in Doctrine and Covenants 89. Eat nutritious food, exercise regularly, and get enough sleep. When you do all these things, you remain free from harmful addictions and have control over your life. You gain the blessings of a healthy body, an alert mind, and the guidance of the Holy Ghost. . . .

"Any drug, chemical, or dangerous practice that is used to produce a sensation or 'high' can destroy your physical, mental, and spiritual well-being. These include hard drugs, prescription or over-the-counter medications that are abused, and household chemicals."[2]

We do not want to harm our mortal bodies, for they are a gift from God, and part of our Heavenly Father's great plan of happiness is the reuniting of our immortal bodies with our spirits.

Another basic necessity is our clothing. A simplified life that brings spiritual blessings requires the wearing of simple and modest clothing. Our dress and grooming send a message to others about who we are, and they also affect the way we act around others. When we are modestly dressed, we also invite the Spirit of the Lord to be a shield and a protection to us.

Worldly trends in women's fashion seem always to

be pushing the extremes. With their latest styles, many fashion designers appear to be trying to make two or three dresses out of the amount of fabric necessary for one. Mostly, they are taking too much off the top and too much off the bottom of women's clothing, and occasionally they scrimp in the middle, too. Men's fashions are also adopting extreme styles. In my day, they would have been called sloppy and inappropriate. I believe very casual dress is almost always followed by very casual manners.

Many of you are trying too hard to be unique in your dress and grooming to attract what the Lord would consider the wrong kind of attention. In the Book of Mormon story of the tree of life, it was the people whose "manner of dress was exceedingly fine" who mocked those who partook of the fruit of the tree. It is sobering to realize that the fashion-conscious mockers in the great and spacious building were responsible for embarrassing many, and those who were ashamed "fell away into forbidden paths and were lost" (1 Nephi 8:27–28).

President N. Eldon Tanner once cautioned us with these words: "Modesty in dress is a quality of mind and heart, born of respect for oneself, one's fellowmen, and the Creator of us all. Modesty reflects an attitude of humility, decency, and propriety. Consistent with these principles and guided by the Holy Spirit, let parents, teachers, and youth discuss the particulars of dress, grooming, and personal appearance, and with free agency accept responsibility and choose the right."[3]

Now let us turn to Thoreau's third requirement, that of shelter. Newspapers are filled with reports of the current housing crisis. At almost every general conference of the Church I can remember, we have been encouraged not to live beyond our means. Our income should determine the kind of housing we can afford, not the neighbor's big home across the street.

President Heber J. Grant once said: "From my earliest recollections, from the days of Brigham Young until now, I have listened to men standing in the pulpit . . . urging the people not to run into debt; and I believe that the great majority of all our troubles today is caused through the failure to carry out that counsel."[4]

One of the better ways to simplify our lives is to follow the counsel we have so often received to live within our income, stay out of debt, and save for a rainy day. We should practice and increase our habits of thrift, industry, economy, and frugality. Members of a well-managed family do not pay interest; they earn it.

Thoreau's final necessity was fuel. We have been hearing a lot about fuel and energy—about their high cost and limited supply, our unsafe and unpredictable dependence on their suppliers, and the need for new and sustainable sources of energy. I leave the discussion of these complicated issues to leaders of government and industry. The fuel I want to discuss is spiritual fuel.

The Lord has given us a beautiful plan about how we can return to Him, but the completion of our mortal journey requires spiritual fuel. We want to emulate the five wise virgins, who had stored sufficient fuel to accompany the bridegroom when he came (see Matthew 25:6–10). What is required to maintain a sufficient store of spiritual fuel? We must acquire knowledge of God's eternal plan and our role in it, and then by living righteously, surrendering our will to the will of the Lord, we receive the promised blessings.

Elder William R. Bradford taught: "In righteousness

there is great simplicity. In every case that confronts us in life there is either a right way or a wrong way to proceed. If we choose the right way, we are sustained in our actions by the principles of righteousness, in the which there is power from the heavens. If we choose the wrong way and act on that choice, there is no such heavenly promise or power, and we are alone and are destined to fail."[5]

Just before Thoreau died, he was asked if he had made peace with God. He replied, "I was not aware we had ever quarreled."[6]

In our search to obtain relief from the stresses of life, may we earnestly seek ways to simplify our lives. May we comply with the inspired counsel and direction the Lord has given us in the great plan of happiness. May we be worthy to have the companionship of the Holy Ghost and follow the guidance of the Spirit as we navigate this mortal journey. May we prepare ourselves to accomplish the ultimate purpose of this mortal test—to return and live with our Heavenly Father.

Chapter Five

DISCIPLESHIP

My mother was a great delegator. Each Saturday morning as my brothers and sisters and I were growing up, we received housecleaning assignments from her. Her instructions to us had been learned from her mother: "Be certain you clean thoroughly in the corners and along the mopboards. If you are going to miss anything, let it be in the center of the room."

She knew very well if we cleaned the corners, she would never have a problem with what was left in the center of the room. That which is visible to the eye would never be left unclean.

Over the years, my mother's counsel has had enormous application for me in many different ways. It is especially applicable to the task of spiritual housecleaning. The aspects of our lives that are on public display usually take care of themselves because we want to leave the best impression possible. But it is in the hidden corners of our lives, where there are things that only we know about, that we must be particularly thorough to ensure that we are clean.

One of those corners of our lives is in the special attention we give in the area of thoughts. We must continually look out for those idle times when our minds are allowed to wander into territory that should be avoided. In Proverbs we read, "For as he thinketh in his heart, so is he" (Proverbs 23:7). And Jude has written, "Filthy dreamers defile the flesh" (Jude 1:8).

Inescapably our thoughts shape our lives. James Allen has expressed it this way in his book *As a Man Thinketh:*

"As the plant springs from, and could not be without, the seed, so every act of a man springs from the hidden seeds of thought, and could not have appeared without them. This applies equally to those acts called 'spontaneous' and 'unpremeditated' as to those which are deliberately executed. . . .

" . . . In the armory of thought he forges the weapons by which he destroys himself; he also fashions the tools with which he builds for himself heavenly mansions of joy and strength and peace. . . . Between these two extremes are all the grades of character, and man is their maker and master. . . .

"Man is the master of thought, the moulder of character, and the maker and shaper of condition, environment, and destiny."[1]

Then Mr. Allen added: "Let a man radically alter his thoughts, and he will be astonished at the rapid transformation it will effect in the material conditions of his life. Men imagine that thought can be kept secret, but it cannot; it rapidly crystallizes into habit, and habit solidifies into circumstance."[2]

Truly one of the corners we must diligently strive to keep clean is our thoughts. The ideal is to keep our thoughts focused on spiritual things.

Perhaps another corner that can accumulate dust because of neglect pertains to the earnest direction we give to our families. President Spencer W. Kimball highlighted his concerns in these words:

"Our success, individually and as a Church, will largely be determined by how faithfully we focus on living the gospel in the home. Only as we see clearly the responsibilities of each individual and the role of families and homes can we properly understand that priesthood quorums and auxiliary organizations, even wards and stakes, exist primarily to help members live the gospel in the home. Then we can understand that people are more important than programs, and that Church programs should always support and never detract from gospel-centered family activities. . . .

"All should work together to make home a place where we love to be, a place of listening and learning, a place where each member can find mutual love, support, appreciation, and encouragement.

"I repeat that our success, individually and as a Church, will largely [depend on] how faithfully we focus on living the gospel in the home."[3]

My general counsel to you is that we must create regimens that foster spiritual housecleaning—ongoing and continual processes that draw us closer to the Lord our Savior so that we can be numbered among His disciples.

The central purpose of our mortal probation is to prepare to meet God and inherit the blessings He has promised to His worthy children. The Savior set the pattern during His earthly ministry and encouraged those who followed Him to become His disciples.

The following has been written about discipleship: "The word *disciple* comes from the Latin [meaning] a learner. A disciple of Christ is one who is learning to be like Christ—learning to think, to feel, and to act [like] he does. To be a true disciple, to fulfill that learning task, is the most demanding regimen known to man. No other discipline compares . . . in either requirements or rewards. It involves the total transformation of a person from the state of the natural man to that of [a] saint, one who loves the Lord and serves with all of his heart, might, mind, and strength."[4]

The Savior instructed those who would follow Him about the essence of discipleship. He said:

"If any man will come after me, let him deny himself, and take up his cross, and follow me.

"And now for a man to take up his cross, is to deny himself of all ungodliness, and every worldly lust, and keep my commandments.

"Break not my commandments for to save your lives; for whosoever will save his life in this world, shall lose it in the world to come.

"And whosoever will lose his life in this world, for my sake, shall find it in the world to come.

"Therefore, forsake the world, and save your souls" (JST, Matthew 16:25–29).

When the spirit conquers the flesh, the flesh becomes a servant instead of the master. When we have cleaned out the corners of worldliness and are ready to be obedient to the Lord, then we are able to receive His word and keep His commandments.

A dramatic change occurs in the lives of individuals when they dedicate themselves to becoming disciples of the Lord. One of the most vivid examples I can think of from the scriptures is the conversion of young Alma and the change that occurred in his very countenance as he became a disciple of the Lord. Remember, Alma and the sons of Mosiah were numbered among the unbelievers.

Alma was a man of many words and could speak much flattery to the people. He led the people to do all manner of iniquity. He became a great hinderment to the Church, stealing away the hearts of the people and causing much dissension among them.

But due to the humble supplications of his father, an angel appeared to Alma and his friends as they were going about their mischief. Alma was so astonished that he fell to the earth, and the angel commanded him: "Alma, arise and stand forth, for why persecutest thou the church of God? For the Lord hath said: This is my church, and I will establish it; and nothing shall overthrow it, save it is the transgression of my people" (Mosiah 27:13). He was so weak he could not lift his limbs and had to be carried. He was also dumb. He was brought and placed before his father. His father rejoiced and called upon the people to pray for his son.

"And it came to pass after they had fasted and prayed for the space of two days and two nights, the limbs of Alma received their strength, and he stood up and began to speak unto them, bidding them to be of good comfort:

"For, said he, I have repented of my sins, and have

been redeemed of the Lord; behold I am born of the Spirit" (Mosiah 27:23–24).

Then he recounted the great tribulation and suffering he went through as he realized he was cast off from the kingdom of God. He remembered the teachings of his father and cried unto the Lord that he might be spared.

Now we see the dramatic change as he becomes a disciple of our Redeemer:

"And now it came to pass that Alma began from this time forward to teach the people, and those who were with Alma at the time the angel appeared unto them, traveling round about through all the land, publishing to all the people the things which they had heard and seen, and preaching the word of God in much tribulation" (Mosiah 27:32).

In my family's pioneer history are many accounts of noble souls who demonstrated the traits of true discipleship. My children's great-grandfather was a valiant disciple of Jesus Christ. Members of his family were wealthy landowners in Denmark. As the favored son, he was to inherit the land of his father. He fell in love with a beautiful young woman who was not of the same social standing as his family. He was encouraged not to pursue the relationship. He was not inclined to follow his family's counsel, and on one of his visits to see her he discovered that all of her family had joined the Church. He refused to listen to the doctrine her family had embraced and forcefully told her that she had to choose between him and the Church. She boldly declared that she would not give up her religion.

Hearing that assured pronouncement, he decided he should listen to the teachings that were so important to her. Soon after, he was touched by the Spirit, and he, too, became converted to the gospel. But when he informed his parents of his decision to join the Church and marry this young woman, they were angry with him and forced him to decide between his family with their wealth and the Church. He walked away from the comforts he had known all of his life, joined the Church, and married the young woman.

Immediately, they started to prepare to leave Denmark and journey to Zion. Now without the support of his family, he had to work hard at any employment he could find to save for the journey to the new land. After a year of hard labor, he had saved enough for their passage. As soon as they were prepared to leave, their branch president went to them and said there was a family with greater need than he and his wife. He was asked to give up what he had saved so the needy family could go to Zion.

Discipleship requires sacrifice. They gave up their savings to the needy family, and then they began another year of hard labor to save to finance their journey. Eventually they arrived in Zion, but not before they had made many more sacrifices, showing true discipleship.

A rich young man was given the harshest test of discipleship when he was told, "Sell all that thou hast, and distribute unto the poor . . . : and come, follow me" (Luke 18:22).

For many of us, an equally challenging test is to shed our bad habits and worldly thoughts so that we are unconflicted and uncompromised in our devotion to the Lord's service.

As true disciples of Christ, may our lives reflect His example. May we take upon ourselves His name and stand as witnesses of Him at all times and in all places (see Mosiah 18:9).

May God bless us to earnestly desire to do our spiritual housecleaning by getting into all the corners and cleaning out all those things that would diminish us as a disciple of the Lord, so that we can move forward in our service to Him who is our King and Savior.

NOTES

CHAPTER 1
HUSBANDS AND FATHERS—
YOUR ROLES AND RESPONSIBILITIES

Adapted from Elder Perry's address in the October 1977 general conference, "Father—Your Role, Your Responsibility," *Ensign,* November 1977, 62–64.

1. David O. McKay, *Gospel Ideals* (Salt Lake City: Improvement Era, 1953), 449.

2. Emma Rae McKay, quoted in *The Savior, the Priesthood, and You* [Melchizedek Priesthood manual, 1973–74] (Salt Lake City: The Church of Jesus Christ of Latter-day Saints, 1973), 207–8.

3. Bryant S. Hinckley, quoted in *The Savior, the Priesthood, and You,* 226.

Chapter 2
Called of God

Adapted from Elder Perry's address in the October 2002 general conference, "Called of God," *Ensign,* November 2002, 7–10.

1. "The Family: A Proclamation to the World," *Ensign,* November 1995, 102.
2. John Taylor, "On Priesthood," *Improvement Era,* June 1935, 372.
3. Stephen L Richards, in Conference Report, October 1938, 118.
4. Spencer W. Kimball, *Marriage* (Salt Lake City: Deseret Book, 1978), 40–41. From the address entitled "Marriage and Divorce" delivered by President Kimball at Brigham Young University, Provo, Utah, 7 September 1976.
5. Brigham Young, *Discourses of Brigham Young,* sel. John A. Widtsoe (Salt Lake City: Deseret Book, 1954), 130.

Chapter 3
The Importance of the Family

Adapted from Elder Perry's address in the April 2003 general conference, "The Importance of the Family," *Ensign,* May 2003, 40–43.

1. See "The Family: A Proclamation to the World," *Ensign,* November 1995, 102.
2. *Gospel Principles* (Salt Lake City: The Church of Jesus Christ of Latter-day Saints, 1997), 231.
3. "Suggestions for Individual and Family Sabbath-Day Activities," *Ensign,* March 1980, 76.

4. Interview, *Boston Globe,* 14 August 2000, quoted in Gordon B. Hinckley, "Family Home Evening," *Ensign,* March 2003, 3.

5. Quoted in Hinckley, "Family Home Evening," 4.

CHAPTER 4

LET HIM DO IT WITH SIMPLICITY

Adapted from Elder Perry's address in the October 2008 general conference, "Let Him Do It with Simplicity," *Ensign,* November 2008, 7–10.

1. Robert Browning, "Rabbi Ben Ezra," in Charles W. Eliot, ed., *The Harvard Classics,* 51 vols. (New York: P. F. Collier & Son, 1909–17), 42:1148.

2. *For the Strength of Youth* (Salt Lake City: The Church of Jesus Christ of Latter-day Saints, 2001), 36–37.

3. N. Eldon Tanner, "Friend to Friend," *Friend,* June 1971, 3.

4. Heber J. Grant, in Conference Report, October 1921, 3.

5. William R. Bradford, "Righteousness," *Ensign,* November 1999, 85.

6. Quoted in Mardy Grothe, comp., *Viva la Repartee* (New York: Collins, 2005), 181.

CHAPTER 5

DISCIPLESHIP

Adapted from Elder Perry's address in the October 2000 general conference, "Discipleship," *Ensign,* November 2000, 60–62.

1. James Allen, *As a Man Thinketh and Other Writings* (Stillwell, Kans.: Digireads.com, 2005), 5–6.

2. Allen, *As a Man Thinketh,* 10.

NOTES

3. Spencer W. Kimball, "Living the Gospel in the Home," *Ensign,* May 1978, 101.

4. Chauncey C. Riddle, "Becoming a Disciple," *Ensign,* September 1974, 81.

ABOUT THE AUTHOR

LOWELL TOM PERRY is a member of the Quorum of the Twelve Apostles of The Church of Jesus Christ of Latter-day Saints. He was ordained an Apostle on 11 April 1974 at the age of fifty-one. A native of Logan, Utah, he received his B.A. in finance from Utah State University. Prior to his call as a General Authority, Elder Perry was president of the Boston Massachusetts Stake and vice president and treasurer of a large chain of department stores. He and his wife, the late Virginia Lee, are the parents of three children. Virginia Perry passed away in December 1974. Elder Perry married Barbara Dayton in 1976.